Letters on Happiness
An Epicurean Dialogue

Peter Saint-Andre

Published by the Monadnock Valley Press,
Parker, Colorado
http://www.monadnock.net/

Cover image by Hans Hillewaert

ISBN: 0615825214

ISBN-13: 978-0615825212

Letters on
Happiness

1

Dear Paul,

How are you, my friend? I hope this note finds you well and happy!

I've been doing some fascinating reading of late. Continuing a theme I mentioned not long ago, my recent focus has been philosophical poetry, which tends to center on issues of happiness and the good life. It's lighter than the real philosophy you and I used to work our way through back in college, but also more approachable — think of pieces like "carpe diem" by Horace or many poems by Walt Whitman.

My current project is in the same vein but a bit heavier: *The Nature of Things*, a very long didactic poem by Lucretius. I've never encountered anything like it! In essence it was an attempt by Lucretius to convert his friend Memmius to the philosophy of Epicurus, which he did by writing a detailed exposition of Epicurean physics and cosmology, with some ethical advice sprinkled throughout. So now of course I'm getting interested in Epicureanism, too. :-)

Have you read much Epicurus? I don't recall much about him from our ancient philosophy class because Professor Rosenbaum was so focused on Plato and the Stoics. These days Epicurus is assumed to be an unthinking hedonist, but perhaps there's more to him than I had realized. Among other things, he appears to have seen a strong link between friendship and happiness, so he wasn't exactly a self-absorbed narcissist. For instance, here's a great quote that someone I follow online posted the other day:

> Friendship dances around the world, announcing to each of us that we must awaken to happiness.

After all, what is more human than the warm connection you feel with someone you are close to? Interestingly — or strangely, depending on your perspective — he focuses on the chosen ties of friendship, not the unchosen ties of family (Nietzsche contrasts the two somewhere in *Human, All Too Human*). Personally I don't see a conflict between the two, but then I've always enjoyed most of my family interactions. Yet I tend to think that friendship is becoming more and more important as people have smaller families, move farther from home, etc.

I'll send along some more thoughts about Epicurus and Lucretius soon.

Your friend,

Schuyler

2

Hey Schuyler,

I've never read Lucretius and it's been a while since I've looked at Epicurus. Even then I was reading about the scientific topics that Lucretius presumably covers, such as the Epicurean doctrine of the atomic swerve (I've always thought that "Epicurus and the Atomic Swerve" would be a great name for a band!). More seriously, it seems that Epicurus and Lucretius anticipated many of the results of modern science: the atomic basis of physics and chemistry and biology, the infinity of the universe, the commonality of physical laws throughout all of nature, the plurality of worlds, even the likelihood of intelligent beings on other planets. As I recall from the history of science, the atomism of Epicurus and Lucretius influenced scientists like Isaac Newton and Robert Boyle (the founder of chemistry) via earlier thinkers such as Pierre Gassendi, Francis Bacon, and Giordano Bruno. It's amazing that Epicurus and Lucretius had these insights 2000 years before the Scientific Revolution!

Since you're reading Lucretius now, shall we explore Epicureanism together? I found a recent translation of many Epicurean maxims on the web, so we could work our way through that and you could report on your reading of Lucretius. Here's the website about Epicurus:

http://www.monadnock.net/epicurus/

As to the link between friendship and happiness, that was a common theme among the ancient Greeks: as you probably remember, Aristotle devoted two whole books of his *Ethics* to friendship, and really it goes all the way back to Homer (think of Achilles and Patroclus). However, it seems that Epicurus might have put a slightly different spin on things, since he emphasized both the pragmatic and emotional benefits of close personal relationships:

> Every friendship is an excellence in itself, even though it begins in mutual advantage. (Vatican Saying 23)

> The use of friends is not that they are useful, but that we can trust in their usefulness. (Vatican Saying 34)

> A friend is not one who is constantly seeking some benefit, nor one who never connects friendship with utility; for the former trades kindness for compensation, while the latter cuts off all hope for the future. (Vatican Saying 39)

I'm out of time for now because I'm in the middle of a big research project at the lab, but I look forward to hearing more about your thoughts on Lucretius. And please let me know if you get a chance to read more of Epicurus. I'll try to read and reflect on a few of his maxims a day (at least they are short and sweet).

—Paul

3

Hi Paul,

Thanks for sending those quotes. I've bookmarked that website and will check it out in detail soon. One thing I noticed right away is that these brief aphorisms are really just the few scraps that remain from the longer works that Epicurus wrote. It might not be easy to reconstruct his philosophy from these scattered fragments, which is where Lucretius might help us out because as far as I can tell he was quite comprehensive in his presentation of Epicureanism. (By the way, I know you're not a huge poetry fan but if you decide to read Lucretius I cannot recommend highly enough the translation by A.E. Stallings, it is absolutely gorgeous!)

On the topic of friendship, I've noticed that in several of his aphorisms Epicurus mentions how your worries about the future can be eased by the trust you have in your friends and by the attention they give to you. Here are a few others in addition the one you quoted about the usefulness of friends:

> All those who have the power to obtain the greatest confidence from their neighbors also live with each other most enjoyably in the most steadfast trust; and

experiencing the strongest fellowship they do not lament as pitiful the untimely end of those who pass away. (Principal Doctrine 40)

We sympathize with our friends not through lamentation but through thoughtful attention. (Vatican Saying 66)

One consideration here seems to be his view that dreadful things are few and short-lived:

The same judgment produces confidence that dreadful things are not everlasting, and that security amidst the limited number of dreadful things is most easily achieved through friendship. (Principal Doctrine 28)

In other words, he seems to think that on those rare occasions when bad things do happen, your friends can fill the gap without being overly burdened.

Does that interpretation sound right to you?

—Schuyler

4

Dear Schuyler,

Yes, Epicurus does seem to think that life is simple and happiness is easy:

Praise be to blessed Nature: she has made what is necessary easy to get, and what is not easy to get unnecessary. (Fragment 469)

As far as I can see this all hinges on his view of what is truly necessary in life, which is "not much":

> The body cries out to not be hungry, not be thirsty, not be cold. Anyone who has these things, and who is confident of continuing to have them, can rival the gods for happiness. (Vatican Saying 33)

Essentially, he holds that if the lack of something causes you pain, then it is a necessary part of life, whereas if not then it is superfluous, idle, trifling, and unnecessary. There are many passages on this topic, as you've probably noticed. Here are a few...

> The desires that do not bring pain when they go unfulfilled are not necessary; indeed they are easy to reject when they are hard to achieve or when they seem to produce harm. (Principal Doctrine 26)

> Among desires, some are natural and necessary, some are natural and unnecessary, and some are unnatural and unnecessary (arising instead from groundless opinion). (Principal Doctrine 29)

> Among natural desires, those that do not bring pain when unfulfilled and that require intense exertion arise from groundless opinion; and such desires fail to be stamped out not by nature but because of the groundless opinions of humankind. (Principal Doctrine 30)

> To those who are able to reason it out, the highest and surest joy is found in the stable health of the body and a firm confidence in keeping it. (Fragment 68)

I'm not convinced of this position yet, but I'll give it some more thought before I post again.

Your friend,

Paul

5

Hi Paul!

OK, let me see if I understand this.

According to Epicurus, only two things are needed for complete happiness: bodily health and peace of mind. Nothing else is necessary to produce the greatest joy — not fame, not wealth, not power, not material luxuries, nothing. The desire for bodily health and peace of mind is natural and necessary, as are the activities and things that support body and soul (food and drink, shelter, clothing, and apparently also higher-order goods like friendship). The desire for anything more is either unnecessary or entirely artificial, and gaining such "additions" does not increase your joy in living, it only embellishes that joy.

Lucretius says something similar early in Book Two of *The Nature of Things*:

> Don't you know it's plain
> That all your nature yelps for is a body free from pain,
> And, to enjoy pleasure, a mind removed from fear and
>   care?
> And so we see the body's needs are altogether spare—
> Only the bare minimum to keep suffering at bay,
> Yet which can furnish pleasures for us in a wide array.

This viewpoint seems counter-intuitive, to say the least. Don't we all feel happier if we get a raise at work, share a good meal with friends and family, hear a familiar song, and so on? It seems that Epicurus doesn't think so. Doesn't that strike you as a bit strange?

—Schuyler

6

Hey Schuyler, that does seem strange!

I suppose he could have argued that, even if you *feel* happier on such occasions, it's not true that you *are* happier. Yet he doesn't seem to draw a contrast between psychological happiness and actual happiness, between your subjective experience and your objective state of human flourishing (as the Aristotelians might put it). Instead, as you've noted, he says that if you have acquired what is natural and necessary then you're as happy as you can possibly be.

This line of thinking leads to the importance of reasoning out what is indeed natural and necessary:

> As soon as the pain produced by the lack of something is removed, pleasure in the flesh is not increased but only embellished. Yet the limit of enjoyment in the mind is produced by reasoning out these very things and similar things, which once provoked the greatest fears in the mind. (Principal Doctrine 18)

> The flesh assumes that the limits of joy are infinite, and that infinite joy can be produced only through infinite time. But the mind, reasoning out the goal and

limits of the flesh and dissolving fears about eternity, produces a complete way of life and therefore has no need of infinite time; yet the mind does not flee from joy, nor when events cause it to exit from life does it look back as if it has missed any aspect of the best life. (Principal Doctrine 20)

You must reflect on the fundamental goal and everything that is clear, to which opinions are referred; if you do not, all will be full of trouble and confusion. (Principal Doctrine 22)

Insofar as you forget nature, you will find yourself in trouble and create for yourself endless fears and desires. (Fragment 203)

I suppose that to modern ears his advice might sound like a hopeless intellectualism: just think your way to happiness. On the other hand, perhaps such a recommendation wasn't so far-fetched to the founder of a philosophy!

—Paul

7

Hi Paul,

I'm still not sure about his claim that happiness is only embellished beyond a certain baseline, but I think I'm starting to understand his general perspective. Much of it seems to derive from his analogy between philosophy and medicine:

A philosopher's words are empty if they do not heal the suffering of mankind. For just as medicine is useless if it does not remove sickness from the body, so philosophy is useless if it does not remove suffering from the soul. (Fragment 221)

Do not pretend to love and practice wisdom, but love and practice wisdom in reality; for we need not the appearance of health but true health. (Vatican Saying 54)

Lucretius builds on that analogy in Book One of *The Nature of Things*, likening his poetic presentation of Epicureanism to the honey that a doctor uses to sugar-coat bad-tasting medicine!

The Epicurean reasoning seems to be this: because philosophy is the art of healing the soul, there is no greater happiness than removing the diseases of the soul. Indeed, he seems to think that the desire for something more than the baseline leads to all sorts of diseases of the soul, especially pain and fear.

For example, a groundless desire for immortality makes you afraid of death (or perhaps it's the fear of death that leads to a desire for immortality); yet death is a natural fact, and if you accept your own mortality then you will have a love and appreciation for life instead of a fear of death.

Train yourself to hold that death is nothing to us, because good and evil consist in sensation, and death is the removal of sensation. A correct understanding that death is nothing to us makes the mortality of life enjoyable — not because it gives one an unbounded span of time, but because it removes the desire for immortality. There is nothing terrifying in life to one who truly understands that there is nothing terrifying in the absence of life. (Letter to Menoeceus, Section 124)

> Most people shrink from death as the greatest of evils, or else extol it as a release from the evils of life. Yet the wise man does not dishonor life (since he is not set against it) and he is not afraid to stop living (since he does not consider that to be a bad thing). Just as he does not choose the greatest amount of food but the most pleasing food, so he savors not the longest time but the span of time that brings the greatest joy. It is simpleminded to advise a young person to live well and an old person to die well, not only because life is so welcome but also because it is through the very same practices that one both lives well and dies well. (Letter to Menoeceus, Section 126)

In this example, the desire for immortality is a kind of disease of the soul, which can be cured through the ministrations of philosophy. It seems to me that an Epicurean could apply similar reasoning to other aspects of life -- say, showing that the desire for fame is a kind of psychological disorder. (Lucretius goes even farther at the beginning of Book Three by claiming that vices like avarice, ambition, and envy are in large measure caused by the fear of death.) I see hints of that in several of the fragments, but it's not spelled out in detail. Perhaps Epicurus explained it all in his longer treatises, but we'll never know for sure (and I haven't found it yet in Lucretius, although I'm only in the middle of Book Three so far).

Looking forward to hearing your thoughts in the matter.

Best,

Schuyler

8

Hey Schuyler,

I think you're really onto something here. With your insight in mind, I've taken a look at some other passages where he talks about groundless desires for things that are unnatural or unnecessary (it's helpful that these Epicurean fragments are online because it's easy to search through them).

Your example of fame is a good one: it is something unnatural, so if you have a groundless desire for fame then you'll have a corresponding fear of living in obscurity. That combination of desire and fear might lead you to do things that will make you unhappy (say, appear in a reality TV show or something silly like that).

Furthermore, Epicurus sometimes groups several similar phenomena in with the desire for fame, such as desires for riches and power (and, I suppose, corresponding fears of poverty and weakness):

> One will not banish emotional disturbance or arrive at significant joy through great wealth, fame, celebrity, or anything else which is a result of vague and indefinite causes. (Vatican Saying 81)

> Happiness and bliss are produced not by great riches nor vast possessions nor exalted occupations nor positions of power, but rather by calmness of mind, freedom from pain, and a disposition of the soul that sets its limits in accordance with nature. (Fragment 548)

Similarly with the desire, common in ancient city-states like Athens, to be acclaimed and honored by one's fellow citizens (and the corresponding fear of being ignored and disrespected by them):

> The esteem of others is outside our control; we must attend instead to healing ourselves. (Vatican Saying 64)

> Some people want to be well esteemed and widely admired, believing that in this way they will be safe from others; if the life of such people is secure then they have gained its natural benefit, but if not then they have not gained what they sought from the beginning in accordance with what is naturally appropriate. (Principal Doctrine 7)

In all of these cases, there is a dyad of unhealthy desires and fears, which are caused by not understanding what is natural and necessary in life and by unreasonably expecting or hoping for something more than the baseline. (I'm still not clear on what exactly is included in that baseline, but in part I think we're defining it as we go along by seeing what's not included, such as fame, fortune, power, and public honors.)

—Paul

9

Hi Paul!

It's interesting that you should mention the desire for power, because I just finished Book Three of *The Nature of Things*, where Lucretius describes how someone who seeks power is like a real-life Sisyphus who is never satisfied because power itself is an illusion that cannot be relied upon.

In addition to fame, fortune, power, and honor, I've found another major example of these dyads: fear of fate and a corresponding desire for complete control over your life. Although Epicurus and Lucretius both often describe fate in terms of the gods (who in ancient times were believed to actively meddle in human affairs), in more modern terms we could talk about a fear of outside forces such as "the culture" or "the environment" or society at large (and let's not forget that there are still people who believe in things like astrology!). Epicurus discusses this topic at length in his *Letter to Menoeceus*:

> In short, whom do you consider better than someone who holds pious opinions about the gods, who is always fearless in the face of death, who has reasoned out the natural goal of life, and who has understood that the limit of good things is easy to fulfill and easy to achieve, whereas the limit of bad things is either short-lived or cause little pain? Someone who laughs at destiny, which is asserted by some to be the master of all things? For he holds that we are responsible for what we achieve, even though some things happen by necessity, some by chance, and some by our own power, because although necessity is not accountable he sees that chance is unstable whereas the things that are within our power have no other master, so that naturally praise and blame are inseparably connected to them. Indeed he sees that it would be better even to cleave to the myths about the gods (since that leaves some hope of prevailing upon them through worship) than to be subject to the destiny of the scientists (since that way lies an inexorable necessity). And such a man holds that Fate is not a god (as most people believe) because a god does nothing disorderly, and he holds

that Fate is not an uncertain cause because nothing good or bad with respect to a completely happy life is given to men by chance, although it does provide the beginnings of both great goods and great evils. And he considers it better to be rationally unfortunate than irrationally fortunate, since it is better for a beautiful choice to have the wrong results than for an ugly choice to have the right results just by chance. (Letter to Menoeceus, Section 133 ff.)

Here again, although the details might be blurry, the general message is clear: accept that some things are outside your control and take responsibility for what is within your control.

Let's see if I can summarize the diseases of soul that Epicurus describes:

- The fear of oblivion leads to the desire for immortality. Yet the ideal (what is natural and necessary) is not to live forever, but to face death without fear and to enjoy the span of your life on earth.
- The fear of weakness leads to the desire for power. Yet the ideal is not to hold power over other people, but to be strong and effective enough to meet your own needs.
- The fear of poverty leads to greed and the desire for great wealth. Yet the ideal is not to be super-rich, but to have enough material goods to meet your true and natural needs for food, shelter, clothing, companionship, etc.
- The fear of obscurity leads to the desire for fame. Yet the ideal is not being renowned to all the world, but being connected to the people who truly matter to you.

- The fear of being disliked leads to the desire for public honors. Yet the ideal is not to be the recipient of great public esteem, but to have self-respect and to be respected by those you know and admire.
- The fear of being bored or being perceived as ordinary leads to a desire for luxury (fancy things, exciting experiences, and such). Yet the ideal is not continuous stimulation but active engagement with the world around you.
- The fear of being considered inferior leads to envy — the desire that others lose what they have. Yet the ideal is not tearing others down, but accepting and improving yourself.

And I'm probably missing a few other "dyads" here.

I'm sure that entire books have been written about envy, greed, and the desire for power, fame, public honors, and luxury, but it seems to me that Epicurus might have been the first person to analyze these vices in a unified way. That's quite an accomplishment!

Your friend,

Schuyler

10

Dear Schuyler,

Good work! I really like your summary, especially the focus on the positive opposites of fear and groundless desire. I agree with you that there might be a few more dyads lurking within Epicurean analysis. For example:

- The fear of being disappointed leads to anger — the desire that other people act as you want them to. Yet the ideal is not feeling that others must conform to your expectations, but accepting others as they are and maintaining your inner serenity.
- The fear of failure leads to laziness — the desire to get something for nothing. Yet the ideal is not passivity but active confidence in your abilities and the pursuit of self-improvement.

Now that we've got a fairly complete inventory of these diseases of the soul, I've been thinking about the psychological effects of being driven by groundless desires for what is unnatural or unnecessary. Given that one side of each dyad is fear, a clear effect is living in fear instead of having a natural confidence about life:

> I summon you to sustained enjoyment and not to empty and trifling virtues, which destroy your confidence in the fruits of what you have. (Fragment 116)

> To those who are able to reason it out, the highest and surest joy is found in the stable health of the body and a firm confidence in keeping it. (Fragment 68)

> We must not blame the body for the greatest evils nor attribute our troubles to mere circumstance. Instead we seek their cause within the soul: for by giving up every groundless and fleeting desire we give birth to a confidence perfect in itself. (Fragment 445)

> One who needs tomorrow least, most gladly greets the coming day. (Fragment 490)

However, the biggest impact is experiencing life as painful rather than pleasant or joyous, since that ties in with the supposed hedonism of Epicurus (I say "supposed" because it turns out he is far from a mindless pleasure-seeker):

> Our every action is done so that we will not be in pain or fear. (Letter to Menoeceus, Section 128)

> It is not possible to live joyously without also living wisely and beautifully and rightly, nor to live wisely and beautifully and rightly without living joyously; and whoever lacks this cannot live joyously. (Principal Doctrine 5)

> We are born only once and cannot be born twice, and must forever live no more. You don't control tomorrow, yet you postpone joy. Life is ruined by putting things off, and each of us dies without truly living. (Vatican Saying 14)

> The flesh assumes that the limits of joy are infinite, and that infinite joy can be produced only through infinite time. But the mind, reasoning out the goal and limits of the flesh and dissolving fears about eternity, produces a complete way of life and therefore has no need of infinite time; yet the mind does not flee from joy, nor when events cause it to exit from life does it look back as if it has missed any aspect of the best life. (Principal Doctrine 20)

So, as Epicurus sets it up, the choice is fairly stark: if you give in to groundless desires for things that are unnatural or unnecessary, then you will live a life of pain and fear. By contrast, if you stay focused on what is natural and necessary then you will experience joy and a confidence in your ability to live. When he puts it that way, you wonder why anyone would choose to give in to groundless desires.

Up until now I don't see that he has a good account for going astray in that way.

—Paul

P.S. That line you quoted from Epicurus about "the destiny of the scientists" is a bit misleading, because elsewhere he describes why it is important to understand the results of natural science and not be afraid of portents in the sky and such, as ancient people often were:

> If our suspicions about astronomical phenomena and about death were nothing to us and troubled us not at all, and if this were also the case regarding our ignorance about the limits of our pains and desires, then we would have no need for studying what is natural. (Principal Doctrine 11)

> It is impossible for someone who is completely ignorant about nature to wash away his fears about the most important matters if he retains some suspicions about the myths. So it is impossible to experience undiluted enjoyment without studying what is natural. (Principal Doctrine 12)

I couldn't let that misunderstanding of us scientists stand uncorrected. ;-)

11

Dear Paul,

That analysis makes sense to me. I also see some more subtle effects here, although perhaps Epicurus would subsume them under pain and fear or joy and confidence.

Consider what he has to say about trouble and confusion vs. serenity and steadiness:

> One who acts aright is utterly steady and serene, whereas one who goes astray is full of trouble and confusion. (Principal Doctrine 17)

> You must reflect on the fundamental goal and everything that is clear, to which opinions are referred; if you do not, all will be full of trouble and confusion. (Principal Doctrine 22)

> Unhappiness is caused by fears, or by endless and empty desires; but he who is able to rein these in creates for himself a blissful understanding. (Fragment 485)

> Passion for true philosophy destroys every disturbing and troublesome desire. (Fragment 457)

> Insofar as you forget nature, you will find yourself in trouble and create for yourself endless fears and desires. (Fragment 203)

> It is not the young man who is most happy, but the old man who has lived beautifully; for despite being at his very peak the young man stumbles around as if he were of many minds, while the old man has settled into old age as if in a harbor, secure in his gratitude for the good things he was once unsure of. (Vatican Saying 17)

The idea here appears to be that concentrating your thoughts and energies on what is natural and necessary gives you a kind of clarity and singleness of purpose, which makes you calm and grounded. However, if you are always

chasing after those embellishments beyond the baseline
then you will be of many minds and torn between
conflicting desires, which makes you troubled and
confused.

Lucretius makes the point more poetically in Book Two of
The Nature of Things:

> But there is nothing sweeter than to dwell in towers
>   that rise
> On high, serene and fortified with teachings of the
>   wise,
> From which you may peer down upon the others as
>   they stray
> This way and that, seeking the path of life, losing their
>   way:
> The skirmishing of wits, the scramble for renown, the
>   fight,
> Each striving harder than the next, and struggling day
>   and night,
> To climb atop a heap of riches and lay claim to might.
> O miserable minds of men! O hearts that cannot see!
> Beset by such great dangers and in such obscurity
> You spend your little lot of life!

I think this is connected to an interesting observation that
Epicurus makes in the Vatican Sayings:

> For most people, to be quiet is to be numb and to be
> active is to be frenzied. (Vatican Saying 11)

That sounds quite modern, doesn't it? Think of all those
people who are only quiet when their minds are numbed
by drugs or TV or some other narcotic, and who otherwise
live a frenzied, agitated existence. To such people,
Epicurus holds out another possibility: a combination of
mindful serenity and flowing activity. So I think those are

wrong who claim that Epicurus counselled laziness and indolence. In this respect, Thomas Jefferson — who said "I too am an Epicurean" — had it right in his letter to William Short (October 31, 1819):

> I take the liberty of observing that you are not a true disciple of our master Epicurus, in indulging the indolence to which you say you are yielding. One of his canons, you know, was that "the indulgence which prevents a greater pleasure, or produces a greater pain, is to be avoided." Your love of repose will lead, in its progress, to a suspension of healthy exercise, a relaxation of mind, an indifference to everything around you, and finally to a debility of body, and hebetude of mind, the farthest of all things from the happiness which the well-regulated indulgences of Epicurus ensure; fortitude, you know, is one of his four cardinal virtues. That teaches us to meet and surmount difficulties; not to fly from them, like cowards; and to fly, too, in vain, for they will meet and arrest us at every turn of our road.

I admit that Jefferson and I might be stretching the evidence here because there's not much to go on in the remaining fragments of Epicurus, so I'd appreciate hearing from you on this point. However, it seems consistent with how Epicurus lived his own life: after all, he wrote many books of philosophy, started his own school, and founded a vibrant community of likeminded people. That's not exactly the way of a lazy pleasure-seeker!

—Schuyler

12

Dear Schuyler,

While I like the portrait Jefferson paints in that letter, I'm not sure it's fully consistent with the fragments of Epicurus. In particular, I haven't found any statement about "four cardinal virtues" in what we've been reading, or about fortitude as a key concept in Epicureanism (have you seen that in Lucretius?). The idea that comes closest is self-reliance, which Epicurus contrasts with dependence in several places:

> The study of what is natural produces not braggarts nor windbags nor those who show off the culture that most people fight about, but those who are fearless and self-reliant and who value their own good qualities rather than the good things that have come to them from external circumstances. (Vatican Saying 45)

> We hold that self-reliance is a great good — not so that we will always have only a few things but so that if we do not have much we will rejoice in the few things we have, firmly persuaded that those who need luxury the least enjoy it the most, and that everything natural is easily obtained whereas everything groundless is hard to get. (Letter to Menoeceus, Section 130)

> He who follows nature and not groundless opinions is completely self-reliant. With regard to what is enough by nature, everything he owns is a source of wealth; whereas with regard to unlimited desires even the greatest wealth is poverty. (Fragment 202)

Self-reliance is the greatest wealth of all. (Fragment 476)

The greatest fruit of self-reliance is freedom. (Vatican Saying 77)

Here again your suggestion of "the baseline" is lurking in the background, because Epicurus holds that if you limit your desires to what is natural and necessary then you will be fearless and self-reliant, and you will have great natural wealth and personal freedom — whereas if your desires are groundless and unlimited then you will be fearful and dependent, and you will live in true poverty and servitude.

Your friend,

Paul

13

Hi Paul,

That's a good catch about fortitude vs. self-reliance — fortitude sounds like a more martial or Stoic virtue than Epicurus would endorse. In fact he doesn't seem to have been a fan of virtue in general (or at least the traditional virtues):

Beauty and virtue and such are worthy of honor, if they bring joy; but if not then bid them farewell! (Fragment 70)

I summon you to sustained enjoyment and not to empty and trifling virtues, which destroy your

28

confidence in the fruits of what you have. (Fragment 116)

In any case, I think we can agree that Epicurus considered dependence to be yet another effect of giving in to groundless desires. And I think I've found one more such effect: what we might call decadence or corruption or a lack of harmony or a lack of integration. Here are some relevant fragments:

If at all critical times you do not connect each of your actions to the natural goal of life, but instead turn too soon to some other kind of goal in thinking whether to avoid or pursue something, then your thoughts and your actions will not be in harmony. (Principal Doctrine 25)

If the things that produced the delights of those who are decadent washed away the mind's fears about astronomical phenomena and death and suffering, and furthermore if they taught us the limits of our pains and desires, then we would have no complaints against them, since they would be filled with every joy and would contain not a single pain or distress (and that's what is bad). (Principal Doctrine 10)

So when we say that pleasure is the goal, we do not mean the pleasures of decadent people or the enjoyment of sleep, as is believed by those who are ignorant or who don't understand us or who are ill-disposed to us, but to be free from bodily pain and mental disturbance. For a pleasant life is produced not by drinking and endless parties and enjoying boys and women and consuming fish and other delicacies of an extravagant table, but by sober reasoning, searching out the cause of everything we accept or reject, and driving out opinions that cause the greatest trouble in the soul. (Letter to Menoeceus, Section 131)

At this point I think we have a fairly complete catalogue of the diseases of the soul and their effects on one's state of mind: fear instead of confidence, pain and anguish instead of joy and pleasure, confusion instead of clarity, numbness instead of awareness, turmoil and frenzy instead of serenity, dependence instead of self-reliance, decadence and dissolution instead of harmony and integrity. (One fascinating side-note: apparently Lucretius or even Epicurus might have been the source for the "seven deadly sins": lust, gluttony, greed, sloth, anger, envy, and pride. This is mentioned in a footnote to the translation of Lucretius I'm reading, but I haven't yet tracked down the scholarly paper in which this argument first appeared.)

The question now is: what remedies does "Doctor Epicurus" prescribe to cure these ills? The basic idea is nicely outlined by Lucretius at the end of Book Three:

> Thus in this way each man is running from himself, yet still
> Because he clings to that same self, although against his will,
> And clearly can't escape from it, he loathes it; for he's ill
> But doesn't grasp the cause of his disease. Could he but see
> This clear enough, a man would drop everything else, and study
> First to understand the Nature of Things, for his own sake...

—Schuyler

30

14

Hey Schuyler,

Thanks for keeping us on track. Yes, let's pursue his medical analogy and see where it leads.

I agree with you about the fundamental Epicurean medicine: align your life with what is natural and necessary. Presumably, we can discover a more specific remedy for each disease of the soul that Epicurus identifies. As one big example, he spends a lot of time talking about overcoming the fear of death:

> Death is nothing to us; for what has disintegrated lacks awareness, and what lacks awareness is nothing to us. (Principal Doctrine 2)

> Train yourself to hold that death is nothing to us, because good and evil consist in sensation, and death is the removal of sensation. A correct understanding that death is nothing to us makes the mortality of life enjoyable — not because it gives one an unbounded span of time, but because it removes the desire for immortality. There is nothing terrifying in life to one who truly understands that there is nothing terrifying in the absence of life. (Letter to Menoeceus, Section 124)

> Only a fool says that he fears death because it causes pain ahead of time, not because it will cause pain when it comes. For something that causes no trouble when present causes only a groundless pain when merely expected. So death, the most terrifying of evils, is nothing to us, because as long as we exist death is not present, whereas when death is present we do not

exist. It is nothing to those who live (since to them it does not exist) and it is nothing to those who have died (since they no longer exist). (Letter to Menoeceus, Section 125)

Most people shrink from death as the greatest of evils, or else extol it as a release from the evils of life. Yet the wise man does not dishonor life (since he is not set against it) and he is not afraid to stop living (since he does not consider that to be a bad thing). Just as he does not choose the greatest amount of food but the most pleasing food, so he savors not the longest time but the span of time that brings the greatest joy. It is simpleminded to advise a young person to live well and an old person to die well, not only because life is so welcome but also because it is through the very same practices that one both lives well and dies well. (Letter to Menoeceus, Section 126)

So his argument — his remedy — seems to be that if you train yourself to believe that "death is nothing to us" then you won't fear death, you won't be continually troubled by your own mortality, you won't dishonor your life, you won't have a groundless desire to live forever, and you won't believe things and do things that are driven such a groundless desire; instead, you will face the prospect of your own extinction without fear, you will be untroubled about death in your day-to-day existence, you will honor your life, and you will enjoy the span of days that is given to you.

Notice how Epicurus says "train yourself that death is nothing to us" and how he focuses on the practices that enable you to live well and die well. Apparently he thought of philosophy as a kind of mental training, and perhaps he counselled his followers to repeat certain phrases to themselves each day or when they were feeling troubled or

32

when they were about to make a decision. That might account for the brief and often memorable aphorisms we find in the Principal Doctrines and Vatican Sayings.

—Paul

15

Hi Paul,

I like this focus on mental training (it's something you find also in other practical thinkers like Baltasar Gracian, Michel de Montaigne, Henry David Thoreau, and Lin Yutang, all of whom strike me as fairly Epicurean in significant ways). Perhaps we can try to express the Epicurean remedies as actionable guidelines, as he does in Vatican Saying 71:

> Ask this question of every desire: what will happen to me if the object of desire is achieved, and what if not?

As to the remedies themselves, another one is knowing that outside forces do not control you, as opposed to believing that your life is controlled by the gods or other powers. In ancient times, many people believed that the gods directly intervened in human affairs, which is why Epicurus concentrates his argument on such beliefs, as in the following quotes (notice that the first one is Principal Doctrine #1):

> That which is blissful and immortal has no troubles itself, nor does it cause trouble for others, so that it is not affected by anger or gratitude (for all such things come about through weakness). (Principal Doctrine 1)

If our suspicions about astronomical phenomena and about death were nothing to us and troubled us not at all, and if this were also the case regarding our ignorance about the limits of our pains and desires, then we would have no need for studying what is natural. (Principal Doctrine 11)

It is impossible for someone who is completely ignorant about nature to wash away his fears about the most important matters if he retains some suspicions about the myths. So it is impossible to experience undiluted enjoyment without studying what is natural. (Principal Doctrine 12)

It is useless to be safe from other people while retaining suspicions about what is above and below the earth and in general about the infinite unknown. (Principal Doctrine 13)

The things that most people say about the gods are based on false assumptions, not a firm grasp of the facts, because they say that the greatest goods and the greatest harms come from the gods. (Letter to Menoeceus, Section 123)

Here Epicurus emphasizes that you need some knowledge of natural phenomena to stop believing in the myths and fearing the influence of external powers on your life. Lucretius has a similar passage early in Book One of *The Nature of Things*:

> For godhead by its nature must enjoy eternal life
> In utmost peace, removed from us and far from
>   mortal strife,
> Apart from any suffering, apart from any danger,
> Powerful of itself, not needing us, and both a stranger

To our attempts to win it over and untouched by
anger.

I must say that often Epicurus and Lucretius seem quite
modern — I think Epicurus especially would fit quite well
within modern society (Lucretius perhaps not so much
because we've lost that poetic feeling for life). On the
other hand, Epicurus is not in favor of science for the sake
of science as some people might be nowadays: the point of
knowing about nature is to experience undiluted
enjoyment of life.

—Schuyler

16

Hey Schuyler, what's wrong with science for the sake of
science?! :P

Actually I'd go one step further, because a closely related
remedy is understanding human nature (as opposed to
filling your head with groundless opinions about the things
people really need in order to live and be happy). There are
many quotes on this topic in the fragments we've been
reading (e.g., his many statements about natural, unnatural,
necessary, and unnecessary desires), but here are some of
the ones that struck me on a second reading...

Natural wealth is both limited and easy to acquire, but
the riches incited by groundless opinion have no end.
(Principal Doctrine 15)

Don't think it unnatural that when the body cries out,
the soul cries also. The body says don't be hungry,
don't be thirsty, don't be cold. It is difficult for the
soul to prevent these cries, and dangerous for it to

ignore the commands of nature because of attachment to its usual independence. (Fragment 200)

Among natural desires, those that do not bring pain when unfulfilled and that require intense exertion arise from groundless opinion; and such desires fail to be stamped out not by nature but because of the groundless opinions of humankind. (Principal Doctrine 30)

Nature must be persuaded, not forced. And we will persuade nature by fulfilling the necessary desires, and the natural desires too if they cause no harm, but pointedly rejecting the harmful desires. (Vatican Saying 21)

We need pleasure when in pain because of its absence; but when we are not experiencing such pain, and are perceiving stably, then there is no need for pleasure. For it is not the needs of nature which, from without, create harm, but desire driven by groundless opinions. (Fragment 422)

Pain does not consist in being deprived of things, but rather in bearing the avoidable distress caused by groundless opinion. (Fragment 486)

Closely related is acting in accordance with human nature, i.e., not giving in to desires that are unnatural and unnecessary but instead desiring only what is natural and necessary:

Keep in mind that some desires are natural whereas others are groundless; that among the natural desires some are natural and necessary whereas others are merely natural; and that among the necessary desires some are necessary for happiness, some for physical health, and some for life itself. The steady contemplation of these facts enables you to understand everything that you accept or reject in terms of the health of the body and the serenity of the soul, since that is the goal of a completely happy life. Our every action is done so that we will not be in pain or fear. As soon as we achieve this, the soul is released from every storm, since an animal has no other need and must seek nothing else to complete the goodness of body and soul. Thus we need pleasure only when we are in pain caused by its absence; but when we are not in pain then we have no need of pleasure. (Letter to Menoeceus, Section 127)

The desires that do not bring pain when they go unfulfilled are not necessary; indeed they are easy to reject when they are hard to achieve or when they seem to produce harm. (Principal Doctrine 26)

It is rare to find a man who is poor in regard to the aims of nature and rich in groundless desires. For a fool is never satisfied with what he has, but instead is distressed about what he doesn't have. Just as those who are feverish through the evil of their sickness are always thirsty and desiring the opposite of what they should, so those whose souls are in a bad condition are always poor in everything and through their greed fall into ever-changing desires. (Fragment 471)

This is why we say that pleasure is the beginning and the end of a completely happy life. For we recognize it as the primary and innate good, we honor it in everything we accept or reject, and we achieve it if we judge every good thing by the standard of how it affects us. And because this is the primary and inborn good, we do not choose every pleasure. Instead, we pass up many pleasures when we will gain more of what we need from doing so. And we consider many pains to be better than pleasures, if we experience a greater pleasure for a long time from having endured those pains. So every pleasure is a good thing because its nature is favorable to us, yet not every pleasure is to be chosen — just as every pain is a bad thing, yet not every pain is always to be shunned. It is proper to make all these decisions through measuring things side by side and looking at both the advantages and disadvantages, for sometimes we treat a good thing as bad and a bad thing as good. (Letter to Menoeceus, Section 128)

Sorry about the mass of quotes! I won't have time to think about this again until the weekend, but I figured I'd at least share the texts I've found.

Best,

Paul

17

Hi Paul,

Thanks for tracking down those fragments. I certainly don't mind sifting through them, because we can use all the evidence we can find. (By the way, all this talk of pleasure might sound like sensualism, but the web pages we've been referencing make it clear that the ancient Greek word *hedone* could just as well be translated as "joy" or "delight" or "enjoyment" or even our modern sense of "happiness" - any physical, mental, or emotional state that is filled with sweetness.)

Some of those passages echo the one I found about "questioning every desire" (Vatican Saying 71). The questions that Epicurus would ask include "will it require intense exertion to realize this desire?", "will it cause me pain and anguish if this desire goes unfulfilled?", and "is this a desire for something that isn't really necessary for life itself, for physical health, for serenity of soul, or for happiness?" If the answer to any of those questions is no, then the desire is groundless, the thing I'm desiring is unnatural or unnecessary or harmful, and it is best to pointedly reject it.

I suppose there might be an escape hatch here, because you could try to justify a desire for something unnecessary by saying that you just can't rest or won't be happy unless you have that fancy car or impressive house or country club membership or whatever. However, Epicurus would probably consider that a form of rationalization, for several reasons.

First, he was in favor of living simply and being satisfied with a frugal lifestyle, and opposed to the pursuit of extravagance and luxury.

> Living on bread and water, I rejoice in the pleasure of my body and spit upon the pleasures of extravagance, not for what they are but because of the difficulties that follow from them. (Fragment 181)

> Send me a little vessel of cheese, so that I can feast whenever I please. (Fragment 182)

> It is better for you to lie serene upon a bed of straw than to be full of troubles on a golden chair at an overflowing table. (Fragment 207)

Fearing an austere way of life, most people end up
doing things that are exceedingly likely to result in fear.
(Fragment 478)

There is an elegance in simplicity, and one who is
thoughtless resembles one whose feelings run to
excess. (Vatican Saying 63)

Second, he recommended a policy of being grateful
for and satisfied with what you have, instead of always
wanting what you don't have.

Don't ruin the things you have by wanting what you
don't have, but realize that they too are things you
once did wish for. (Vatican Saying 35)

Nothing is enough to one for whom enough is very
little. (Vatican Saying 68)

Misfortune must be cured through gratitude for what
has been lost and the knowledge that it is impossible
to change what has happened. (Vatican Saying 55)

The ingratitude of the soul makes a creature greedy for
endless variation in its way of life. (Vatican Saying 69)

This saying is utterly ungrateful for the good things
one has achieved: provide for the end of a long life.
(Vatican Saying 75)

He who forgets the good things he had yesterday
becomes an old man today. (Vatican Saying 19)

One who perceives the limits of life knows how easy it
is to expel the pain produced by a lack of something
and to make one's entire life complete; so that there is

no need for the things that are achieved through struggle. (Principal Doctrine 21)

Third, I think he would see a desire for "keeping up with the Joneses" as an instance of following the herd or being brainwashed by the culture around you, as opposed to setting your own course in life.

> Embark on your own course: steer clear of all culture. (Fragment 163)

> We cast off common customs just as we would do to wicked men who have been causing great harm for a long time. (Vatican Saying 46)

> Although some measure of safety from others comes from the power to fight them off and from abundant wealth, the purest security comes from solitude and breaking away from the herd. (Principal Doctrine 14)

> Congratulations: you have entered into philosophy free from all culture. (Fragment 117)

> I never wanted to please the many. What pleased them, I did not learn; and what I learned, was beyond their ken. (Fragment 187)

> Speaking freely in my study of what is natural, I prefer to prophesize about what is good for all people, even if no one will understand me, rather than to accept common opinions and thereby reap the showers of praise that fall so freely from the great mass of men. (Vatican Saying 29)

Finally, I think he would see the desire for impressive things as a kind of vanity or crowd-pleasing, in which you seek the esteem of others instead of basing your esteem on your own character and accomplishments.

> The esteem of others is outside our control; we must attend instead to healing ourselves. (Vatican Saying 64)

> Some people want to be well esteemed and widely admired, believing that in this way they will be safe from others; if the life of such people is secure then they have gained its natural benefit, but if not then they have not gained what they sought from the beginning in accordance with what is naturally appropriate. (Principal Doctrine 7)

So I think he has a pretty thorough critique of justifying indulgence in groundless desires as the pursuit of happiness. According to Lucretius at the end of Book Five, it all comes down to living philosophically and being satisfied with little:

> But if you'd steer your life by a philosophy that's true,
> The way to be the wealthiest of men is to eschew
> High living, and be contented in the mind — for there
>   has never
> Been a poverty of modest means...

That said, Epicurus and Lucretius don't seem to provide many positive guidelines about what it means for something to be necessary for happiness or serenity, as opposed more objective phenomena like physical health or life itself.

—Schuyler

18

Dear Schuyler,

I tend to agree on that last point. Not that the failing is limited to Epicurus: plenty of philosophers are better at critiquing other thinkers than in setting forth their own positive views. At least Epicurus offered some practical guidelines of the kind you've distilled from those passages. Good detective work! Let's see if I can help us advance the cause a bit further...

Returning to the concept of remedies for diseases of the soul, I think you've just explained several, because living extravagantly, following the herd, being ungrateful for what you have, and seeking to impress other people all lead to feelings of insecurity. The reason is that these things come from outside of yourself and are outside of your control; whether you have them or not is a matter of good fortune, not your own actions.

> The ignoble soul is inflated by good fortune and deflated by misfortune. (Fragment 488)

> Nature teaches us to think nothing of what fortune brings, to understand that when prospering we are unfortunate and when not prospering we are fortunate, to receive undisturbed the good things that fortune brings and to stand ready for its seeming evils. For what is good or evil to most people is fleeting, and wisdom has nothing in common with fortune. (Fragment 489)

Thus the wise, noble, beautiful soul is not swayed by the winds of fortune or driven by chance events, but instead directs his life by the power of reason.

Chance steals only a bit into the life of a wise person: for throughout the complete span of his life the greatest and most important matters have been, are, and will be directed by the power of reason. (Principal Doctrine 16)

Infinite time and finite time contain the same amount of joy, if its limits are measured out through reasoning. (Principal Doctrine 19)

The flesh assumes that the limits of joy are infinite, and that infinite joy can be produced only through infinite time. But the mind, reasoning out the goal and limits of the flesh and dissolving fears about eternity, produces a complete way of life and therefore has no need of infinite time; yet the mind does not flee from joy, nor when events cause it to exit from life does it look back as if it has missed any aspect of the best life. (Principal Doctrine 20)

What brings unsurpassed joy is the removal of a great evil; and this is the nature of the good, if you apply your mind rightly and then stand firm and do not stroll about chattering emptily. (Fragment 423)

This appeal to a life of reason is stirring, but it's not always clear how to put it into practice. One aspect might be something you've already highlighted: questioning every desire to understand its causes and effects. But clearly people who understand what's right don't always do the right thing. Epicurus has an explanation for that, too:

No one who sees what is bad chooses it willingly; instead he is lured into seeing it as good compared to what is even worse, and thus he is trapped. (Vatican Saying 16)

So an actionable guideline here might be to not compare alternatives only to what is worse, but also to what is better or ideal (that is, what is "natural and necessary").

I'm still not sure how helpful that advice is in reality, though, because the difficult choices are always the messy ones...

Your friend,

Paul

19

Paul, I think you're right: much of what Epicurus regards as rational is in fact tied to his conception of what is natural and necessary. Although we still haven't identified what it means for something to be necessary for happiness, I think we can at least identify some related remedies.

A key idea here is what we earlier referred to as harmony or even a kind of integrity (i.e., being an integrated person whose actions are consistent with his thoughts). Consider again the following maxims:

> It is not the young man who is most happy, but the old man who has lived beautifully; for despite being at his very peak the young man stumbles around as if he were of many minds, whereas the old man has settled into old age as if in a harbor, secure in his gratitude for the good things he was once unsure of. (Vatican Saying 17)

> If at all critical times you do not connect each of your actions to the natural goal of life, but instead turn too

soon to some other kind of goal in thinking whether to avoid or pursue something, then your thoughts and your actions will not be in harmony. (Principal Doctrine 25)

The implication is clear: if you perform that "questioning of your desires" at important times in your life, those questions will lead you to determine whether a given course of action is natural and necessary. However, if during that decision process you turn toward or are trapped by a goal other than what is natural and necessary, you will stumble around in confusion or be of many minds.

Furthermore, the natural goal of life is often a matter of understanding your limits (as Lucretius puts it at the start of Book Six, Epicurus "set a limit to desire and an end to fear"). This is connected to the advice of the ancient oracle at Delphi to know yourself. Here are a few fragments on the topic...

The person who has put together the best means for confidence about external threats is one who has become familiar with what is possible and at least not unfamiliar with what is not possible, but who has not mixed with things where even this could not be managed and who has driven away anything that is not advantageous. (Principal Doctrine 39)

One who perceives the limits of life knows how easy it is to expel the pain produced by a lack of something and to make one's entire life complete; so that there is no need for the things that are achieved through struggle. (Principal Doctrine 21)

And because acting within your limits will make you happy with what you have and what you are, there is no need to be envious or jealous of other people:

> Envy no one. For good people do not deserve envy, and the more that wicked people succeed the more they ruin things for themselves. (Vatican Saying 53)

That all sounds good and reasonable, but I'm not sure how to square it with modern life given everyone's focus on work and earning power and getting ahead. Do you think it's possible to live as an Epicurean today?

Still puzzling over it all,

Schuyler

20

Schuyler, those are searching questions. It does seem that Epicurus would advise his modern-day followers to drop out of the rat race to some extent:

> If you want to make Pythocles wealthy, do not increase his riches but reduce his desires. (Fragment 135)

> Many of those who happen into wealth are not liberated from their troubles but merely swap them for greater ills. (Fragment 479)

> Happiness and bliss are produced not by great riches nor vast possessions nor exalted occupations nor positions of power, but rather by calmness of mind, freedom from pain, and a disposition of the soul that

sets its limits in accordance with nature. (Fragment 548)

Poverty is great wealth if measured by the goals of nature, and wealth is abject poverty if not limited by the goals of nature. (Vatican Saying 25)

A free person is unable to acquire great wealth, because that is not easily achieved without enslavement to the masses or to the powers that be. Instead, he already has everything he needs, and in abundance. But if by chance he should have great wealth, he could easily share that with his fellows to win their goodwill. (Vatican Saying 67)

One will not banish emotional disturbance or arrive at significant joy through great wealth, fame, celebrity, or anything else which is a result of vague and indefinite causes. (Vatican Saying 81)

Here again there's quite a bit of wiggle room. What is "great wealth"? In modern terms, would be OK to achieve a middle-class existence but not strive to become super-rich or really famous? I haven't seen anything in what Epicurus says which would require vows of poverty, and in any case he seems to be more concerned about struggling in the public arena or making yourself a slave to mass opinion or societal authorities. This is connected to the traditional Epicurean advice to avoid public office or involvement in political affairs:

They must free themselves from the prison of public affairs and ordinary concerns. (Vatican Saying 58)

Live unknown. (Fragment 551)

That last fragment is especially cryptic. What does it really mean to live unknown? Clearly Epicurus himself wasn't unknown, and indeed was a somewhat prominent person during his lifetime. After all, we're still talking about him 2500 year later, which is just about the opposite of passing through life in obscurity!

To try to answer your more general question, I would say that at one level it's difficult to apply ancient ideas to life today because our modern existence is so different from how people lived back then. In particular, our society is much more contractual and less based on extended family ties, religious affiliations, authoritarian power, or the kind of philosophical community that Epicurus established at "the Garden" in Athens.

These days I think it's imperative to learn how to thrive in a market economy, continually refine your skills, seek new opportunities, and so on. That kind of dynamism was probably missing from ancient society, so it seems to me that the pursuit of wealth (although perhaps not great or excessive wealth) is almost a personal imperative these days. However, that doesn't mean you need to indulge in groundless desires for more and more material possessions, as so many people do today.

Furthermore, as you noted, Epicurus himself was a hard-working person (he founded a philosophy, wrote many books, etc.). I can only think that he considered the psychological results of all that hard work to be worth it in the end. Such an attitude would be consistent with something he said in the *Letter to Menoeceus*:

> And we consider many pains to be better than pleasures, if we experience a greater pleasure for a long time from having endured those pains. (Letter to Menoeceus, Section 129)

What do you think?

Best,

Paul

21

Paul, I'm no expert on the differences between Hellenistic Greece and modern America, but the contrast you draw rings true with me. Further, Epicurus might have been writing for those who lived in the Garden, which appears to have been a kind of intentional community. We do know that other Epicureans started similar communities for hundreds of years afterward, so perhaps those people were isolated somewhat from the forces of the market economy at the time. However, I would agree that modernity is more atomistic or individualistic than antiquity. In a way, that might make Epicureanism a good fit for people today (for example, his philosophy seems more aligned with modern science than a system like Aristotelianism).

On the other hand, the great economist Ludwig von Mises once observed that the division of labor in modern market economies can be seen as a culmination of the influence of Epicurus:

> The historical role of the theory of the division of labor as elaborated by British political economy from Hume to Ricardo consisted in the complete demolition of all metaphysical doctrines concerning the origin and the operation of social cooperation. It consummated the spiritual, moral and intellectual emancipation of mankind inaugurated by the philosophy of Epicureanism.

So perhaps the case is not so clear-cut.

That said, there might be another connection between Epicurean communities and some aspects of his ethical views, because one remedy he offers for insecurity is treating other people with justice, and he thinks that justice is a kind of compact to not harm the fellow members of one's community (which in the case of the Garden would have been a chosen bond):

> Natural justice is a covenant for mutual benefit, to not harm one another or be harmed. (Principal Doctrine 31)

> Justice does not exist in itself; instead, it is always a compact to not harm one another or be harmed, which is agreed upon by those who gather together at some time and place. (Principal Doctrine 33)

> In general, justice is the same for all: what is mutually advantageous among companions. But with respect to the particulars of a place or other causes, it does not follow that the same thing is just for all. (Principal Doctrine 36)

> One who causes fear cannot be without fear. (Fragment 537)

> The greatest fruit of justice is serenity. (Fragment 519)

Notice his emphasis on the interactions you have with your companions. This really brings us full circle back to friendship, which he elevates to an exalted position among the remedies for unhappiness.

Of all the things that wisdom provides for the complete happiness of one's entire life, by far the greatest is friendship. (Principal Doctrine 27)

The noble soul is devoted most of all to wisdom and to friendship — one a mortal good, the other immortal. (Vatican Saying 78)

The same judgment produces confidence that dreadful things are not everlasting, and that security amidst the limited number of dreadful things is most easily achieved through friendship. (Principal Doctrine 28)

Trying to focus again on practicalities, I'd note that Epicurus also offers some guidelines for friendship, such as doing favors for your friends, making sure that they benefit from their interactions with you, and taking reasonable risks to build and maintain your friendships:

Don't avoid doing small favors, lest you seem to be the same with regard to greater things. (Fragment 214)

Those who grasp after friendship and those who shrink from it are not worthy of approval; on the other hand, it is necessary to risk some pleasure for the pleasures of friendship. (Vatican Saying 28)

A friend is not one who is constantly seeking some benefit, nor one who never connects friendship with utility; for the former trades kindness for compensation, while the latter cuts off all hope for the future. (Vatican Saying 39)

As I mentioned at the beginning of our conversation about Epicurus, his connection between friendship and happiness is very attractive to me (and again somewhat modern because it puts less emphasis on family and more emphasis on your chosen relationships).

Indeed, the connection runs much deeper than a superficial observation that having friends gives you pleasure. Although Lucretius doesn't talk much about friendship in *The Nature of Things*, the entire book is devoted to converting his friend Memmius to Epicureanism — literally to saving the life of his friend, if you agree with Epicurus and Lucretius that true philosophy is the only reliable cure for the diseases of the soul. And notice how Epicurus exhorts his friend Menoeceus to "practice these and similar things day and night, by yourself and with a like-minded friend" — the presence of a friend reinforces your practice of the precepts of true philosophy, and enables you to "live as a god among men" because friendship is an immortal good. These certainly are strong claims for the power of friendship, but Epicurus makes them because the love and practice of wisdom (philosophy in its original sense) is something you can achieve much more easily in collaboration with the people you value most deeply. Kind of like we've been doing together in these letters. :-)

—Schuyler

22

Dear Schuyler,

I too like how Epicurus ties happiness, friendship, and the love of wisdom. As we've seen, he also makes connections to happiness from reason, clarity, beauty, joyfulness, simplicity, serenity, justice, self-reliance, prudence, gratitude, confidence, and courage. And he tries to make it easy to put these insights into practice in everyday life. It's quite an appealing package, even if some of the details are still hazy (and might always remain so, given how little survives of his original writings). You can see why so many people converted to the philosophy of Epicurus in ancient days, and so infrequently converted from Epicureanism to some other creed.

One thing that still puzzles me is this matter of "the baseline", however. Why can't your enjoyment of life be increased instead of merely embellished once you have certain necessities taken care of (food, shelter, companionship, and the like)? I've been pondering that the whole time we've been exchanging these messages, and I think I might have a path toward the answer.

In essence, although perhaps he didn't express it very well, I think that Epicurus had a reverence for life — he felt a simple joy in being alive and in being conscious of himself and the beauty of existence, and to him this pleasure was strong and sweet and utterly basic and irreducibly individual. So to him, everything above that was mere embellishment: as long as he was alive and healthy and not threatened by cold or hunger or worried about where his next meal was coming from, he felt perfectly happy because the very fact of being alive was precious and beautiful.

Now, I grant that this is speculation and maybe it's something more poetic than he was comfortable saying directly, but it's the only way I can make sense of his idea of the baseline and his non-hedonistic view about the pleasure of living.

I'm curious to hear what you think about this hypothesis.

—Paul

23

Hi Paul!

That insight rings strikes a chord with me, but then I'm a poet at heart. It does seem more emotional or spiritual than Epicurus might have been comfortable with — my impression from his fragments is that he was a bit dry in how he expressed things — but I think it's consistent with his somewhat strange ideas about pleasure and happiness.

It seems to me that it might be easier to capture this spiritual aspect of Epicureanism in poetry than in prose. As Lucretius wrote to start Book Five of *The Nature of Things*:

> Who can build a fitting song, who has the strength of heart
> To match the Majesty of Things and these truths in his art?

Indeed, throughout the centuries, numerous fine poets — Horace, Catullus, Shelley, Tennyson, Swinburne, Whitman, Dickinson, Pessoa, and of course our friend Lucretius — have been influenced by Epicurus in his emphasis on tranquility, understanding nature, avoiding politics, and enjoying each day. As a matter of fact, I recently noticed that the person who made the Epicurus translation we've been using has rendered some of the more Epicurean poems of Horace into English (see http://www.monadnock.net/horace/). He has also written an original poem entitled "In The Garden", which captures many of the themes we've been discussing all this time. I thought I'd send it along for your enjoyment...

In the garden of my life
I'm done with envy, done with strife.
I cultivate my natural joys
Far from this culture's fearful noise.

Congress hall and marketplace,
Fame's small change and honor's race,
Academe's cold, haughty tower
Have no meaning, hold no power.

Letting go of shoulds and oughts,
I concentrate on greener thoughts
And find as I fulfill my soul
That things spin calmly in control —

That though events conspire still,
They tend to bend toward my will.
No greater cause achieves the measure
Than that of my own reasoned pleasure.

Paul, it's been a true pleasure exploring Epicurus and Lucretius with you, and I hope you've enjoyed it as much as I have!

Your friend,

Schuyler

24

Dear Schuyler,

Thanks for sending that poem — it does a good job of capturing the Epicurean sense of life in contemporary language (and it's certainly a quicker read than Lucretius!).

Speaking of brief summaries, I've discovered an ancient recipe for happiness according to Epicurus, called the "tetrapharmakos" or four-part cure:

> Don't fear god.
> Don't worry about death.
> What's good is easy to get.
> What's bad is easy to bear.

It doesn't get much simpler than that, does it? Although we have picked up some more particular advice along the way, the four-part cure really cuts to the essence and is quite memorable (as Epicurus noted in the Vatican Sayings, "short discourses and long discourses both achieve the same thing").

I know I've certainly enjoyed our discourse about Epicurus, too! Let's do it again sometime. ;-)

Your friend,

Paul

THE END

For Further Exploration

The Roman poet Lucretius wrote a long poem on Epicurean philosophy entitled *The Nature of Things*, which A.E. Stallings has beautifully translated into English recently (hers is the version I quote from in the dialogue). Another ancient poet influenced by Epicurus was Horace, whose most Epicurean-minded poems I have translated in my collection *Ancient Fire*. Additional poets of a somewhat Epicurean bent include Catullus, Tennyson, Swinburne, and Pessoa.

Both *The Epicurus Reader* and *The Essential Epicurus* provide English versions of the few writings of Epicurus that survive from antiquity. My own translations of his (even fewer) works on the topic of the good life can be found at http://www.monadnock.net/epicurus/ along with notes on the texts.

A broad Epicurean community flourished for seven hundred years in ancient times. Of late, his ideas have experienced a resurgence of interest among those seeking meaning in modern life. Various websites, discussion lists, and forums are available for learning and interaction. Although I lack the time to engage with them all, I have found them uniformly welcoming and blessedly free of the unhealthy obsession with political matters that so infects the culture we live in.

If you have questions, comments, or suggestions for improving this book, feel free to contact me via the means posted at my personal website, https://stpeter.im/

Made in the USA
Middletown, DE
23 July 2018